Linda Brogan

What's in the Cat

D0928795

Methuen Drama

Published by Methuen 2005

1 3 5 7 9 10 8 6 4 2

First published in 2005 by
Methuen Publishing Limited
11–12 Buckingham Gate
London SW1E 6LB

Methuen Publishing Limited Reg. No. 3543167

A CIP catalogue record for this book is available from
the British Library

ISBN 0 413 77577 1

Typeset by Country Setting, Kingsdown, Kent
Printed and bound in Great Britain by
Bookmarque Ltd, Croydon, Surrey

ROYAL COURT

The Royal Court presents the Contact production of

WHAT'S IN THE CAT
by Linda Brogan

First performance at Contact Theatre, Manchester on 18 November 2005, and at
The Royal Court Jerwood Theatre Upstairs, Sloane Square, London on 7 December 2005.

WHAT'S IN THE CAT

by **Linda Brogan**

Cast
Lauren **Rachel Brogan**
Peter **Curtis Cole**
Margaret **Mary Jo Randle**
Bogey **David Webber**
Lee **Geoff Aymer**

Director **Paulette Randall**
Designer **Libby Watson**
Lighting Designer **James Farncombe**
Sound Designer **Dan Steele**
Casting **Gaby Kester**
Production Manager **Chris Whitwood**
Stage Managers **Emma Cook, Martin Fuller**
Wardrobe Supervisor **Jacquie Davies**
Set Builder **The Workhaus**
Fight Director **Andy Quine**
Scenic Artist **Emily Campbell**

THE COMPANY

Linda Brogan (writer)
Theatre includes: You Are What You Eat, The Very Thought of You (Wolseley/Tricyle); Basil and Beattie (Royal Exchange/Liverpool Everyman); Ghost Town (Clean Break); Black Crows, The Well (Contact). Radio includes: God Can See Down Entries. Awards include: NWP Anniversary Commission 2003 (for Basil and Beattie), Lefeurve/Promis Prize, Alfred Fagon Award 2001, Bolton Festival Shorts 2001(for The Well), BBC Northern Exposure Awards 2001(for What's in the Cat).

Geoff Aymer
Theatre includes: The Big Life (Apollo/Theatre Royal Stratford East); Henry IV (Etcetera); Revolution, Evolution (Edinburgh/Cockpit/Canal Café); Pantheon of the Gods, Hamlet, Macbeth (Young Vic); The Wiz, As The Chicken Jerks (Hackney Empire); Newrevue (Canal Café).

Rachel Brogan
For the Royal Court: Redundant.
Theatre includes: Port, The Sanctuary Lamp, Dog Boy (Manchester Royal Exchange); Iron (Manchester Contact Theatre); Street Trilogy (Theatre Absolute UK tour).
Television includes: Doctors, Casualty, Twisted Tales, Blue Murder.
Radio includes: Canned, Falling, No Harm.

Curtis Cole
Curtis graduated from the HNC Theatre course in July 2004. Since then he has worked for WWP production company on a trilogy of three short films. Curtis is a young writer in residence at Contact 2005. This is his professional theatre debut.

James Farncombe (lighting designer)
For the Royal Court: Blest Be The Tie.
Other theatre includes: Nathan the Wise, Osama the Hero, A Single Act (Hampstead); The Maths Tutor (Hampstead Theatre/Birmingham Rep) ;Street Trilogy (Car, Raw and Kid), Cloudburst (Theatre Absolute); Playboy of the West Indies (Tricycle/Nottingham Playhouse); Blues for Mr Charlie (Tricycle/Ipswich Wolsey); Improbable Fiction (directed by Alan Ayckbourn), Making Waves, Soap (Stephen Joseph Theatre, Scarborough); The Price, Larkin with Women (Library Theatre, Manchester); Hysteria (Northcott, Exeter); Forward The Door, Birmingham Rep);

High Heel Parrotfish, Urban Afro Saxons, Funny Black Women on the Edge Theatre (Royal Stratford East); This Lime Tree Bower (The Belgrade, Coventry); To Kill a Mockingbird, Master Harold and the Boys, West Side Story, Death of a Salesman, Peter Pan, The Witches, Plague of Innocence, Unsuitable Girls (Leicester Haymarket Theatre); The Hypochondriac (nominated Manchester Evening News Awards Best Design Team 2003) Popcorn and The Twits (Bolton Octagon); Amy's View (Salisbury Playhouse/Royal Theatre, Northampton); Beautiful Thing (Nottingham Playhouse/national tour); Abigail's Party(York Theatre Royal); Dead Funny (York Theatre Royal/ Bolton Octagon); Krapp's Last Tape, A Who's Who of Flapland, A Different Way Home, A Visit From Miss Prothero (Lakeside Arts Centre, Nottingham); Lord of the Flies, Bloodtide, Road, Rumblefish (Pilot Theatre Company/York Theatre Royal/national tour); The Blue Room, The Elephant Man (Worcester Swan Theatre); Unsuitable Girls (Sheffield Crucible Studio/tour); East is East, A Women of No Importance (New Vic Theatre Stoke); Goldilocks (Lyric Theatre, Hammersmith); Mignon, The Merchant of Venice (Guildhall). Projects for 2006 include Mustapha Matura's new adaptation of Three Sisters at Birmingham Rep and Alan Ayckbourne's Improbable Fiction at the Yvonne Arnaud in Guildford prior to national tour.

Paulette Randall (director)
For the Royal Court: Blest Be the Tie (& Talawa).
For Talawa TC, theatre includes: Urban Afro Saxons, High Heel Parrotfish (Theatre Royal Stratford East); Abena's Stupidest Mistake (Drill Hall); Blues For Mr Charlie (New Wolsey Ipswich/Tricycle). Other theatre includes: King Headley II (Tricycle/ Birmingham Rep); Funny Black Women on the Edge, Shoot to Win, various Posse shows; Two Trains Running, Up Against the Wall (Tricycle); The Amen Corner (Bristol Old Vic); Sanctuary (Joint Stock); For Colored Girls Who Have Considered Suicide When the Rainbow is Enuf (BAC/ Albany Empire); Moon on a Rainbow Shawl (Nottingham). Television includes: Kerching!, Desmond's, The Real McCoy, Porkpie, Marvin, Comin' Atcha (two series), Blouse and Skirt, The Crouches, Little Miss Jocelyn. Paulette is Chair of the Board of Clean Break Theatre Company and was the Artistic Director of Talawa Theatre Company from 2003-05.

Mary Jo Randle

Theatre includes: The Memory of Water (Hampstead); Divine Right (Birmingham Rep); Renegades (Bristol Old Vic); Phaedra (Lyric, Hammersmith); Question Time (Yvonne Arnaud/Arcola); The Public (Theatre Royal, Stratford East); Dearly Beloved, Releevo (Soho); Steaming (Haymarket Theatre, Leicester); Yorkshire Tragedy (National Theatre Studio Workshop); The Changeling, The Alchemist (Crucible Theatre, Sheffield); Top Girls, On the Razzle (Leeds Playhouse); Educating Rita (Belgrade Theatre, Coventry); Les Liaisons Dangereuses, Troilus and Cressida, Philistines, As You Like It (RSC); A View From the Bridge, A Midsummer Night's Dream, Twelfth Night, Macbeth (New Victoria Theatre, Stoke).

Television includes: Pierrepoint, The Royal, The Baby War, Natasha, Midsomer Murders, Gifted, Doctors, Between the Sheets, Holby City, Cutting It, Cambridge Spies, Heartbeat, Holby City, Casualty, The Lakes, Born To Run, The Bill, Bad Behaviour, Between the Lines, Ruth Rendell Mysteries, Van Der Valk, Sister Wife, A Time To Dance, Ex, Olly's Prison, Eastenders, Inspector Morse, Act of Will, London's Burning, Victoria Wood - As Seen on TV, Shine on Harvey Moon, Further Adventures of Dominic Hyde.

Dan Steele (sound designer)

Theatre includes: Hamlet, Rosencrantz and Guildenstern are Dead (English Touring Theatre); Grace (Quarantine); Mona (Nitro Theatre Company); Once Upon a Time in Wigan (Urban Expansions) 13 Mics/B Like Water (Contact/Benji Reid Company); Mania (Michael Mayhew Company); You Hang Up First, Under My Skin, Bad Reputations, Smilin' Through, BRO:9, Perfect (Contact)

Awards include: Best Design in 2003 for BRO:9 and Best Design 2004 for Perfect.

Dan also runs sound workshops in schools and has taught audio production techniques.

Libby Watson (designer)

For the Royal Court: Blest Be the Tie (Royal Court). Other theatre includes: 12 Angry Men, Monday After the Miracle, Othello, Sisterly Feelings, Corpus Christ, Merchant of Venice (Guildhall); Hysteria and Man of Mode (Northcott); Urban Afro Saxons, Funny Black Women, High Heel Parrotfish, The Oddest Couple and Cinderella (Stratford East;) Blues for Mr Charlie, Under their Influence (Tricycle) Effie May (Oval House); Vengeance, The Comedian, Accelerate, Call to the Sky, Mr and Mrs Schultz, Gigolo, I dreamt I Dwelt in Marble Halls Call to the Sky, Lone Flyer, Witch and The Garden at LLangoed (Watermill); Sus (Greenwich Theatre); Airport 2000 (Leicester Haymarket/ Riverside Studios).

As resident designer at Salisbury Playhouse, Beautiful Thing, The Changeling, Tenant of Wildfell Hall, Secret Garden and Arabian Nights.

Opera: Comedy on the Bridge, Beatrice and Benedict and Mignon,

Future projects: Gem of the Ocean (Tricycle), Three Sisters, Deranged Marriage (Leicester Haymarket/tour).

Libby Watson trained at Wimbledon School of Art

David Webber

Theatre includes: The Big Life (Apollo), Master Harold & The Boys (Bristol Old Vic/Southwark); Othello(Good Company), Mrs Sweet (Theatre Royal, Stratford East); Hiawatha, One Love, The Bassett Table (Bristol Old Vic); Two Tracks & Text Me, Ticket to Write, The Beatification of Area Boy (West Yorkshire Playhouse/world tour); Flyin' West, The Looking Glass, King Lear, The Lion, Smile Orange, The Road, Antony & Cleopatra (Talawa/ Kingston, Jamaica tour); Leave Taking (RNT); Downfall (Contact); The Merchant of Venice (Manchester Library); No One Writes to the Colonel (Lyric, Hammersmith); Death & The King's Horseman (Manchester Royal Exchange); Ragamuffin (Double Edge); The Colored Museum (Hackney Empire/tour); Remembrance (Tricycle/Carib, London).

Television includes: Funland, Doctors, Eastenders, Grass, Holby City, London's Burning, The Bill, Homie & Away, The Knock, Accused, Prime Suspect V, 2 Point 4 Children, Coronation Street, The Brittas Empire, The Taming of The Shrew.

Film includes: London Voodoo, All or Nothin, Tipping the Velvet, 51st State, Among Giants, The Avengers, Getting Hurt.

Contact is Manchester's pioneering theatre for young people. Re-opened in 1999, with a new vision of what theatre can be, our mission is to make and produce ground-breaking performance by and for young adults (13-30). Located off Oxford Road, Manchester, Contact is a space that welcomes artists, participants, audiences and visitors from many different backgrounds.

With participation at the organisation's core, we programme an extensive and exciting range of work with a focus on young people. Year-round we bring together a wealth of emerging theatre, new writing, international work, UK based touring theatre companies and home-grown productions. In our participatory, emerging and professional work we mix drama, dance, multi-media, spoken word, comedy, slams, club nights, events, exhibitions, showcases, poetry, physical theatre, hip-hop, film, live art and debates, to explore what theatre can be.

In 2003, Linda was Contact's Writer in Residence. It is during this residency that she developed further ideas for 'What's in the Cat'. Both the concept commission and Linda Brogan's residency at Contact were funded by the BBC's Northern Exposure Programme. Contact continues to support and develop writers from a wide range of ages and disciplines through its RAW- Rhythm and Words, new writing programme.

Contact's previous productions include: 'Unsuitable Girls', 'Wise Guys', 'Vurt', 'Somewhere the Shadow', 'Storm', 'You Hang Up First', 'BRO:9', 'Perfect' and 'Smilin' Through'.

For more information about Contact please visit our website: www.contact-theatre.org

Contact is supported by
The Association of Greater Manchester Authorities
Manchester City Council
Arts Council England
The University of Manchester

To find out more about RAW, Contact's new writing programme, please email
raw@contact-theatre.org.uk

Contact, Oxford Road, Manchester M15 6JA
Contact is a Registered Charity
number 501953
www.contact-theatre.org.uk

THE ENGLISH STAGE COMPANY AT THE ROYAL COURT

The English Stage Company at the Royal Court opened in 1956 as a subsidised theatre producing new British plays, international plays and some classical revivals.

The first artistic director George Devine aimed to create a writers' theatre, 'a place where the dramatist is acknowledged as the fundamental creative force in the theatre and where the play is more important than the actors, the director, the designer'. The urgent need was to find a contemporary style in which the play, the acting, direction and design are all combined. He believed that 'the battle will be a long one to continue to create the right conditions for writers to work in'.

Devine aimed to discover 'hard-hitting, uncompromising writers whose plays are stimulating, provocative and exciting'. The Royal Court production of John Osborne's Look Back in Anger in May 1956 is now seen as the decisive starting point of modern British drama and the policy created a new generation of British playwrights. The first wave included John Osborne, Arnold Wesker, John Arden, Ann Jellicoe, N F Simpson and Edward Bond. Early seasons included new international plays by Bertolt Brecht, Eugène Ionesco, Samuel Beckett, Jean-Paul Sartre and Marguerite Duras.

The theatre started with the 400-seat proscenium arch Theatre Downstairs, and in 1969 opened a second theatre, the 60-seat studio Theatre Upstairs. Some productions transfer to the West End, such as Terry Johnson's Hitchcock Blonde, Caryl Churchill's Far Away and Conor McPherson's The Weir. Recent touring productions include Sarah Kane's 4.48 Psychosis (US tour) and Ché Walker's Flesh Wound (Galway Arts Festival). The Royal Court also co-produces plays which transfer to the West End or tour internationally, such as Conor McPherson's Shining City (with Gate Theatre, Dublin), Sebastian Barry's The Steward of Christendom and Mark Ravenhill's Shopping and Fucking (with Out of Joint), Martin McDonagh's The Beauty Queen Of Leenane (with Druid), Ayub Khan Din's East is East (with Tamasha).

Since 1994 the Royal Court's artistic policy has again been vigorously directed to finding and producing a new generation of playwrights. The writers include Joe Penhall, Rebecca Prichard, Michael Wynne, Nick Grosso, Judy Upton, Meredith Oakes, Sarah Kane, Anthony Neilson,

photo: Andy Chopping

Judith Johnson, James Stock, Jez Butterworth, Marina Carr, Phyllis Nagy, Simon Block, Martin McDonagh, Mark Ravenhill, Ayub Khan Din, Tamantha Hammerschlag, Jess Walters, Ché Walker, Conor McPherson, Simon Stephens, Richard Bean, Roy Williams, Gary Mitchell, Mick Mahoney, Rebecca Gilman, Christopher Shinn, Kia Corthron, David Gieselmann, Marius von Mayenburg, David Eldridge, Leo Butler, Zinnie Harris, Grae Cleugh, Roland Schimmelpfennig, Chloe Moss, DeObia Oparei, Enda Walsh, Vassily Sigarev, the Presnyakov Brothers, Marcos Barbosa, Lucy Prebble, John Donnelly, Clare Pollard, Robin French, Elyzabeth Gregory Wilder, Rob Evans, Laura Wade and Debbie Tucker Green. This expanded programme of new plays has been made possible through the support of A.S.K. Theater Projects and the Skirball Foundation, The Jerwood Charity, the American Friends of the Royal Court Theatre and (in 1994/5 and 1999) in association with the National Theatre Studio.

In recent years there have been record-breaking productions at the box office, with capacity houses for Joe Penhall's Dumb Show, Conor McPherson's Shining City, Roy Williams' Fallout and Terry Johnson's Hitchcock Blonde.

The refurbished theatre in Sloane Square opened in February 2000, with a policy still inspired by the first artistic director George Devine. The Royal Court is an international theatre for new plays and new playwrights, and the work shapes contemporary drama in Britain and overseas.

AWARDS FOR
THE ROYAL COURT

Jez Butterworth won the 1995 George Devine Award, the Writers' Guild New Writer of the Year Award, the Evening Standard Award for Most Promising Playwright and the Olivier Award for Best Comedy for Mojo.

The Royal Court was the overall winner of the 1995 Prudential Award for the Arts for creativity, excellence, innovation and accessibility. The Royal Court Theatre Upstairs won the 1995 Peter Brook Empty Space Award for innovation and excellence in theatre.

Michael Wynne won the 1996 Meyer-Whitworth Award for The Knocky. Martin McDonagh won the 1996 George Devine Award, the 1996 Writers' Guild Best Fringe Play Award, the 1996 Critics' Circle Award and the 1996 Evening Standard Award for Most Promising Playwright for The Beauty Queen of Leenane. Marina Carr won the 19th Susan Smith Blackburn Prize (1996/7) for Portia Coughlan. Conor McPherson won the 1997 George Devine Award, the 1997 Critics' Circle Award and the 1997 Evening Standard Award for Most Promising Playwright for The Weir. Ayub Khan Din won the 1997 Writers' Guild Awards for Best West End Play and New Writer of the Year and the 1996 John Whiting Award for East is East (co-production with Tamasha).

Martin McDonagh's The Beauty Queen of Leenane (co-production with Druid Theatre Company) won four 1998 Tony Awards including Garry Hynes for Best Director. Eugene Ionesco's The Chairs (co-production with Theatre de Complicite) was nominated for six Tony awards. David Hare won the 1998 Time Out Live Award for Outstanding Achievement and six awards in New York including the Drama League, Drama Desk and New York Critics Circle Award for Via Dolorosa. Sarah Kane won the 1998 Arts Foundation Fellowship in Playwriting. Rebecca Prichard won the 1998 Critics' Circle Award for Most Promising Playwright for Yard Gal (co-production with Clean Break).

Conor McPherson won the 1999 Olivier Award for Best New Play for The Weir. The Royal Court won the 1999 ITI Award for Excellence in International Theatre. Sarah Kane's Cleansed was judged Best Foreign Language Play in 1999 by Theater Heute in Germany. Gary Mitchell won the 1999 Pearson Best Play Award for Trust. Rebecca Gilman was joint winner of the 1999 George Devine Award and won the 1999 Evening Standard Award for Most Promising Playwright for The Glory of Living

In 1999, the Royal Court won the European theatre prize New Theatrical Realities, presented at Taormina Arte in Sicily, for its efforts in recent years in discovering and producing the work of young British dramatists.

Roy Williams and Gary Mitchell were joint winners of the George Devine Award 2000 for Most Promising Playwright for Lift Off and The Force of Change respectively. At the Barclays Theatre Awards 2000 presented by the TMA, Richard Wilson won the Best Director Award for David Gieselmann's Mr Kolpert and Jeremy Herbert won the Best Designer Award for Sarah Kane's 4.48 Psychosis. Gary Mitchell won the Evening Standard's Charles Wintour Award 2000 for Most Promising Playwright for The Force of Change. Stephen Jeffreys' I Just Stopped by to See the Man won an AT&T: On Stage Award 2000.

David Eldridge's Under the Blue Sky won the Time Out Live Award 2001 for Best New Play in the West End. Leo Butler won the George Devine Award 2001 for Most Promising Playwright for Redundant. Roy Williams won the Evening Standard's Charles Wintour Award 2001 for Most Promising Playwright for Clubland. Grae Cleugh won the 2001 Olivier Award for Most Promising Playwright for Fucking Games. Richard Bean was joint winner of the George Devine Award 2002 for Most Promising Playwright for Under the Whaleback. Caryl Churchill won the 2002 Evening Standard Award for Best New Play for A Number. Vassily Sigarev won the 2002 Evening Standard Charles Wintour Award for Most Promising Playwright for Plasticine. Ian MacNeil won the 2002 Evening Standard Award for Best Design for A Number and Plasticine. Peter Gill won the 2002 Critics' Circle Award for Best New Play for The York Realist (English Touring Theatre). Ché Walker won the 2003 George Devine Award for Most Promising Playwright for Flesh Wound. Lucy Prebble won the 2003 Critics' Circle Award and the 2004 George Devine Award for Most Promising Playwright, and the TMA Theatre Award 2004 for Best New Play for The Sugar Syndrome. Linda Bassett won the 2004 TMA Theatre Award for Best Actress (for Leo Butler's Lucky Dog).

ROYAL COURT BOOKSHOP

The Royal Court bookshop offers a range of contemporary plays and publications on the theor and practice of modern drama. The staff specialise in assisting with the selection of audition monologues and scenes. Royal Court playtexts from past and present productions cost £2.
The Bookshop is situated in the downstairs

ROYAL COURT BAR
Monday–Friday 3–10pm, Saturday 2.30–10pm
For information tel: 020 7565 5024
or email: bookshop@royalcourttheatre.com

PROGRAMME SUPPORTERS

The Royal Court (English Stage Company Ltd) receives its principal funding from Arts Council England, London. It is also supported financially by a wide range of private companies, charitable and public bodies, and earns the remainder of its income from the box office and its own trading activities.

The Genesis Foundation supports the Royal Court's work with International Playwrights

The Jerwood Charity supports new plays by new playwrights through the Jerwood New Playwrights series.

The Skirball Foundation funds a Playwrights' Programme at the theatre. The Artistic Director's Chair is supported by a lead grant from The Peter Jay Sharp Foundation, contributing to the activities of the Artistic Director's office. Bloomberg Mondays, the Royal Court's reduced price ticket scheme, is supported by Bloomberg. Over the past nine years the BBC has supported the Gerald Chapman Fund for directors.

THE AMERICAN FRIENDS OF THE ROYAL COURT THEATRE

AFRCT supports the mission of the Royal Court and are primarily focused on raising funds to enable the theatre to produce new work by emerging American writers. Since this not-for-profit organisation was founded in 1997, AFRCT has contributed to ten productions. It has also supported the participation of young artists in the Royal Court's acclaimed International Residency.

If you would like to support the ongoing work of the Royal Court, please contact the Development Department on 020 7565 5050.

SLOANE SQUARE

12 January–11 February 2006
Jerwood Theatre Downstairs

Royal Court and Out of Joint present

O GO MY MAN
by **Stella Feehily**

director **Max Stafford-Clark**
designer **Es Devlin**
lighting **Johanna Town**
sound **Gareth Fry**

cast: **Paul Hickey, Denise Gough, Sam Graham, Susan Lynch, Aoife McMahon, Gemma Reeves, Mossie Smith, Ewan Stewart**

Supported by
JERWOOD NEW PLAYWRIGHTS

15–18 February 2006
Jerwood Theatre Downstairs

Guildhall School of Music & Drama presents

LIVE LIKE PIGS
by **John Arden**

director **Christian Burgess**
design **Agnes Treplin**
lighting **Johanna Town**
composer **Julian Philips**

LIVE LIKE PIGS was originally directed by George Devine and Anthony Page at the Royal Court in 1958.

BOX OFFICE
020 7565 5000
BOOK ONLINE
www.royalcourttheatre.com

For Peggy and Bas

with thanks to John E. McGrath

What's in the Cat

Characters

THE LAWRENCE FAMILY

Margaret, *mother, Irish, forty-eight*
Lauren, *daughter, mixed race, fifteen*
Bogey, *father, Jamaican, fifty*
Peter, *son, mixed race, twelve*
Lee, *uncle, Jamaican, fifty-five*

Setting

*Christmas morning and afternoon, 1974. Downstairs in the Lawrences'
clean, stark terraced house in Moss Side. The set comprises:*

*Slim hallway: exterior side wall with wall-mounted family coat rack
with coats; back wall with front door and interior side wall with door
leading into living room.*

*Living room: shared hallway wall with Bogey's armchair, next to the
back wall with central chimney breast with fire. Tinsel Christmas tree
on top of sixties television and brand new Chopper bike propped up
against its side. Shared kitchen wall with door leading into kitchen.
Folded down drop-leaf oak dining table. Centre stage: oblong teak coffee
table in front of fire, shared by both the free-standing sofa and Bogey's
armchair. Central overhead light with paper Christmas decorations to
each corner of the room.*

*Galley kitchen: exterior side wall with stone sink encased in wooden
cupboard, Formica table used as worktop, cooker, fifties upright Formica
kitchen dresser with drop-down worktop, plastic vegetable rack, pots,
pans, food.*

Christmas evening, 1974.

*As before, except the top of the hallway, closest to audience, is now the
corner of Bogey and Margaret's bedroom featuring a back wall with
pink candlewick-spread-covered double bed, a pink bedside lamp, a
seventies radio, a hairbrush and a large canister of hairspray on a
bedside cupboard next to bed. Bedroom door leading to landing. Exterior
side wall with fifties veneered double wardrobe. The door of Bogey's
side is open, hangers still there, but his clothes are gone. The mirror on
the inside of the door reflects the double bed and the upright, battered,
brown Jamaican grip on the floor. Central: a small bedroom rug.*

Act One

Morning.

Margaret *and* **Lauren** *come through the front door.*

Margaret   Come in. Come in, lovey.

Peter *is lying on the floor of the living room in front of the fire, watching the end of a religious morning service on TV. His half-eaten selection box is on the coffee table beside him.*

Margaret *and* **Lauren** *enter. It's been raining.*

Lauren *puts her dad's present on the folded-down dining table behind his chair.*

Margaret *takes her damp headscarf off her newly set, tight-permed hair, shakes it out, then drapes it across the mantelpiece. She turns the gas fire down.*

Margaret (*to* **Peter**)   D'you want him to kill you altogether? Take your coat off, lovey. At least have a cup of tea. Come and get a warm. (*On her way to kitchen, passing the new bike.*) Boy, there's sly and there's sly.

Peter   He was buying me a bike anyway.

Margaret   Who said you can open it?

Peter   He doesn't care.

Margaret   He cares far more than we give him credit for. (*Going into the kitchen.*) Useless raw-mouthed bitch. All she's used to is sitting with her legs wide open in the bit of dirt they call 'mi yard' – seeing who she can attract next.

Margaret *takes her huge bottle of Guinness from the cupboard under the sink and fills her oversized tea mug. Then hides the bottle back under the sink. She goes back to the living room.*

Peter (*taking a parcel from under the tree*)   I know what this is.

Margaret   You best stop shaking it, then.

We hear the toilet flush upstairs.

Margaret   Sit down, Lauren.

We hear the sink taps upstairs running. Then gargling.

Margaret (*re* **Peter** *and TV*)   Turn that shit off. Lauren, stay where you are.

Bogey *is coming downstairs.*

Margaret *goes back in the kitchen. She puts the kettle on.*

Peter   Bonzo's dead.

Bogey *comes through the living-room door.*

Margaret *gets her Guinness out again. Pours – drinks – hides the bottle back under the sink.*

Peter   Someone chopped him with an axe.

Bogey, *ignoring* **Lauren**, *turns the fire up and stands in front of it, warming the backs of his legs for ages.*

He sits in his chair by the fire.

He takes his whiskey out of the drop-leaf table's cupboard. He pours a capful into his hands and washes his head with it.

He holds his cap in front of the fire to warm it.

He puts his whiskey back in the cupboard and turns the fire down.

Bogey   Turn the telly up.

Margaret *enters the living room with a cup of tea for* **Bogey** *and one for* **Lauren**.

Bogey   What you call that?

Margaret   You've packed yours.

Bogey   You know everything I do. Peter, go for me cup.

Margaret   You can see he's watching his programme.

Bogey   You no hear me – go for me cup.

Bogey *gives* **Peter** *the key to his suitcase.*

Peter *goes upstairs.*

Margaret *goes for plain biscuits for* **Bogey** *and chocolate biscuits for* **Lauren** *from the kitchen.*

Margaret   Take your coat off, Lauren. Sit down.

Peter *comes running back down the stairs with* **Bogey**'s *enamel mug.*

Bogey   Where you find it?

Peter   On top of where you put it.

Bogey   You lock it back?

Bogey *slams the enamel mug on the drop-leaf table and slides it cowboy-style to* **Margaret**.

Margaret   Twelve months that took me to pay for, but of course that don't have to worry you.

Margaret *goes back into the kitchen to pour* **Bogey**'s *tea into his mug.*

Lauren *is still by the door.*

Bogey   I don't like him at all as Jason.

Peter   It's the same guy every year.

Bogey   Him with the beard, I like.

Margaret   Must be why he's stopped shaving.

She comes in with the new tea.

They've got the fool on pills now. Show her your happy pills. Lives the fucking life of Riley. What's he got to be depressed about? Pacing for months – this is the welcome you give her.

Bogey   When it suits you – you find her. Move outta the way a the television.

Lauren   Mum said you haven't been well.

Margaret   They'll be giving him a fucking Oscar next. They drop pickney like flies where he sprang from. I'll tell you his problem, shall I?

Lauren   Mum, leave it.

Margaret   The bastard's been eating like a horse. You forget, mister, it's me who puts the rubbish out.

Bogey   Turn the telly up, Peter.

Margaret   What yer gonna do when you get there, hey – and the chimp tells you to kiss her big black behind? Mind, eighteen years won't be a problem for her, Lauren, love. They expect them to bed anything that walks. Big black arses cocked at every veranda. And these lot sniffing. Dogs on heat is all they are.

Bogey   You know everything.

Margaret   I know what's troubling you, matey. Your little pale prize over there – hey – this white blood didn't progress him none. Shame and pride's pecking over his bones this very fucking minute.

Peter   Shhh now. Dad, it's the bit with the skeletons.

Margaret *slams back into the kitchen. She gets out her Guinness, has another drink, hides the bottle.*

Peter   Can we open our presents now?

Bogey   You can do what you like for me.

Lauren *goes into the kitchen to her mum.*

Margaret   D'you want some eggs or summat?

Lauren   I'm not hungry.

Margaret   What about the thing inside yer?

Lauren   I can't eat if I can smell it.

Margaret   Lauren don't think of others – do you, Lauren? Lauren only ever thinks of Lauren.

Lauren   D'you want me to do owt?

Margaret (*drinking her Guinness*)   He might fall for your game.

Lauren *goes back in the living room.*

Lauren   Dad, I'm going.

No reply.

I'm going back to do me exams. I just wanted you to know. They've found me a place with a crèche.

Margaret (*shouting from kitchen*)   A mother-and-baby home, she means.

Lauren   A school unit with a crèche. It's a real nice place, Dad. The new part, the crèche, the baby part is dead bright. My bit's like a posh old school.

Lauren *opens the living-room door to leave.*

Bogey   When your body's ripe there's no shame in bearing pickney – you hear me.

Pause.

Only murder itself would make me turn you away from me door.

Pause.

I thought you knew me long time.

Lauren   Poppa, I'm sorry.

Bogey   We're all sorry – but sorry don't sorry for we.

Margaret *gets behind the kitchen door to listen.*

Bogey   I don't know if you're dead, to raase. Or walking the streets naked. (*Pause.*) I don't work every hour God send to watch harm come to either of unnu.

Peter *turns round and is staring at his dad.*

Bogey   Me have five pickney home who want what you have.

Peter *looks back at the TV.*

Bogey   As long as me and you is on the same land it's my door you knock on, not strangers. (*Pause.*) Awake night after night a worry.

Lauren *goes into the kitchen to her mum.*

Margaret *wipes* **Lauren***'s tears with the tea towel.*

Margaret   Why d'you do these things to yourself, Lauren? It breaks my heart to see you like this. There's no man prouder than he was of you. When he came in from work − who was it he looked for?

Lauren   I know.

Margaret   He doesn't trust many people, Lauren.

Lauren   I know.

Margaret   All you've done is satisfy them who were waiting for you to fall. Take your coat off. If there weren't girls willing to be fields they couldn't sow their wild oats.

Margaret *helps* **Lauren** *take off her coat.*

Margaret   Don't bring up the boy or any of that stuff, you hear me. You hear me? If it was a white boy maybe. You know how he is. Keep your eye on the turkey. I'll be back down, just let me take this thing off. (*Re hospital uniform − taking* **Lauren***'s coat with her.*)

Lauren   What's that funny smell?

Margaret   I can't smell anything. Mind, I was the same having you. I'll be down soon.

Margaret *passes through the living room to get changed. She hangs* **Lauren***'s coat up in the hallway.*

Peter (*pulling his dad's pyjama bottoms as* **Bogey** *nods off*)   *King Kong*'s on soon.

Margaret   Leave him, he hasn't slept proper for weeks. (*Calling back to* **Lauren** *re* **Peter**.) His fucking eyes'll fall out of his head one day soon. Knowing him he'll step on one of them.

Lauren (*checking the turkey*)   Knowing him he'll step on both of 'em.

Blackout.

Afternoon.

Bogey *is still asleep in his chair by the fire.*

Lauren's *on the sofa.*

Peter *is lying on his stomach on the floor in front of the fire, watching the TV.*

Having changed into a cardy and skirt and put on some lippy and face powder, **Margaret** *is in the kitchen pouring a sly glass of Guinness from her big bottle into her oversized tea mug. She hides the bottle back under the sink. She gets the turkey out and bastes it.*

Margaret   Is he coming to do his rice?

Lauren   She's shouting you. Dad, she's shouting yer.

Bogey *wakes up, bewildered.*

Lauren   Me mam's shouting yer.

Margaret   Come and do this if you're doing it. I've enough to do.

Lauren   What's that smell?

Margaret   What smell?

Lauren   Burning plastic.

Margaret   Ask him if he's not planning to eat with us.

Bogey   Tell her I'm coming.

Bogey *takes his bottle of whiskey from the cupboard. He pours a capful, takes off his cap and washes his head with it. Puts the whiskey back.*

He takes his spare jumper from the back of his chair and warms it in front of the fire.

He takes his spare socks from the arm of his chair. Knocking **Margaret**'s *headscarf off the mantelpiece, he warms the socks in front of the fire, puts them on over his existing socks.*

Puts on his slippers, starts walking towards the kitchen.

Lauren   The lights have just gone out.

Margaret   What?

Lauren   The tree.

Margaret   If he's waiting for me to put this on.

Lauren   He's coming. Pete, move out the way of the telly.

Peter   You're not even watching.

Lauren   How would you know?

Lauren *moves to* **Bogey**'s *chair by the fire.*

Margaret   Start again and see what happens.

Bogey *arrives in the kitchen.*

Margaret   The Iceman cometh.

Margaret *gets the rice out of the cupboard and gives it to* **Bogey**.

Bogey *puts the rice in a pan and starts washing it furiously under a running tap.*

Margaret   Summat'll get you in the end, Big Man.

Bogey   Move outta me way.

Bogey *turns the cooker on full belt, putting the pan of rice straight on it.*

Margaret   Turn it down. You have the arse burnt out of all me pans.

Bogey   Peter, where's the salt me buy?

Margaret   Right there in front of you.

Living room.

Lauren   D'you wanna play Mousetrap?

Peter   I missed that now through you.

Lauren   This is over in a minute.

Peter   *King Kong*'s on after this.

Margaret   Come and do the sprouts if you're looking for something to do.

Lauren   Let him do 'em.

Margaret   He's watching his film.

Bogey   Move outta me way.

Lauren   The kitchen's freezing.

Margaret   Get King Farouk here to put his hand in his pocket.

Peter   Leave 'em while they're quiet.

Lauren   Shut up, you.

A knock at the front door.

Margaret   Who the fuck's that now?

Lauren   I'm not getting it.

Peter   It's the last minutes.

Lauren   I'm not getting it.

Another knock at the front door.

Margaret   Will one of you get the door?

Lauren   Let him do summat.

Bogey   Lauren – get the door.

Peter *grins at* **Lauren**.

Lauren   You've just missed the last minutes, dickhead.

Bogey   Get the door – you don't hear me?

Margaret   His Master's Voice.

Peter *turns the TV up.* **Lauren** *gets up from the couch. She goes to the front door.*

Margaret (*shouting from kitchen*)   Don't think you're going out that door, Peter. For Christ's sake, will you turn that pan down? Look at the state of the stove now.

Lauren *opens the door.*

Lauren   Brother Lee.

Lee   Lady Lauren returns. (*Kisses his teeth in disgust.*) Tell your father I want him.

Lauren   Come in outta the rain.

Lee   Tell him it won't take a minute.

Margaret *comes through to the living room on her way to the kitchen.*

Margaret   Who is it?

Lauren   Brother Lee for me dad.

Margaret *comes into the hallway.*

Margaret   Come in outta the rain.

Lee   Just a little word with Bogey, me want, Margaret. I won't disturb you.

Margaret   He's done enough rice to feed half of China. We're having the full issue if you'd prefer.

Lee   Just get your father, Lauren.

Margaret   It's not bad news, is it?

Lee   Nuttin to worry your head about. Lauren –

Margaret   He knows you're here. Take your coat off at least. The other night –

Lauren (*shouts through to* **Bogey**)   Lee's here.

Bogey *walks through to the hallway.*

Bogey   Me know.

Lauren   Why didn't you answer then?

Bogey   You think cos your belly's big. Come upstairs, man.

Lauren *goes back to* **Bogey**'s *chair.*

Bogey *and* **Lee** *go upstairs.*

Margaret *is left in the hallway on her own. Trying to listen to them upstairs, she starts messing with the coats and shoes in the hallway.*

Lauren (*shouting to* **Margaret**)   There's a right smell coming from the kitchen.

Margaret   Well, go and see what it is then. I can't smell anything. Pete, can you smell anything?

Peter *doesn't answer.*

Lauren   The Quality Street are still upstairs.

Peter   Shut up.

Lauren   And the ham. D'you want me to get 'em out the bottom of the wardrobe?

Margaret   I'll go meself.

Lauren   I bet you will.

Margaret *goes back to the kitchen.*

Peter   You're fucking evil, you.

Margaret *gets her Guinness out again. Pours herself another mugful. Hides bottle.*

Lauren   Mum, if that's ginger beer, I'll have some.

Peter *stares at* **Lauren**.

Lauren   You've missed another minute.

Peter   Why don't you piss off back to that hostel?

Lauren   Why don't you drop dead?

Peter   We're all right without you.

Lauren   Really. Is that why she came begging this morning?

Margaret *pours two glasses of ginger beer from the flagon under the sink, brings them in.*

Margaret   It's not fetch me carry me all day. I didn't get you in that state.

Peter   She doesn't know who did.

Margaret   Watch your mouth.

Peter   Lauren – the bike.

Margaret   What's got into yer?

Lauren   I thought you were going for the sweets.

Peter   I'll go.

Margaret   I'll go meself when I'm ready.

Lauren   Pete wants the triangles. Don't yer, Pete?

Peter   You wanna see the stuff on the gable end about her, Mam.

Lauren   You better shut the fuck up.

Margaret   Talk like that in this house again.

Peter   Any time – any place – anywhere.

Lauren   You'd better shut him up.

Peter   You shouldn't have done it, girl. You just shouldn't have done it.

Lauren   He only stays in school to get his fucking mark.

Peter   I'm outside Cunningham's office every fucking dinner.

Lauren   You don't say nowt to him, I notice.

Margaret   Shhh!

Bogey and **Lee** *are coming downstairs.*

As **Bogey** *opens the front door for* **Lee**, **Margaret** *rushes into the hallway.*

Margaret   Lee, we've got more than enough. What's the use in you being on your own?

Bogey   You go long, man.

Margaret   You gave me the whiskey.

Bogey   I gave it you?

Margaret   You didn't stop me.

Bogey   You can't stop yourself?

Margaret   Come on, you stubborn old git. I'll give you only white meat.

Bogey   You go on, sir.

Lee   Again tonight and I won't darken this door –

Margaret   Take your coat off, you daft fucker. It's me you're talking to.

Bogey   You stand there a think it's free food you're getting. (*Kisses his teeth.*)

Margaret   Take no notice of him. He's always been a miserable fucker. (*To* **Bogey**.) Shake your head all you want – your brother knows already.

Margaret *helps* **Lee** *take his coat off.*

Lee   Fool I'm fool.

Lauren   A hungry cunt you mean.

Margaret   Which one of you said that?

Lauren   It'd hardly be him.

Margaret   When you drop that thing inside you, every last thing you've meted out will come back. And then I'll laugh me bollocks off.

Lauren   Then me dad can have 'em back.

Margaret *goes to hit her.*

Lauren   All you're good for.

Margaret   At least I was married.

Lauren   Pity you couldn't stay that way.

Margaret   A great pity – I'd have never given birth to the likes of you.

Bogey This is what you kept the man for?

Margaret Who wanted her back here?

Bogey I wouldn't see a dog without a home on Christmas day.

Margaret She had all the kennel she needed.

Bogey Lauren, when your pain start it's that woman you'll call out for. Don't make no smart remark. What was clever about you, you dashed away already.

Margaret You want a whiskey, Lee? Don't worry, I'm not gonna touch a drop today. I've not had a drink all day, have I, Bogey?

Lauren Except the ginger beer under the sink.

Bogey Pete, move your foot, let Lee pass. You're gonna ruin your eyes.

Lauren With what he's up to morning, noon and night, it's a wonder he's not blind.

Bogey Go upstairs.

Lee You have any pale ale?

Lauren Check under the sink.

Bogey Go upstairs.

Lauren Look if you don't believe me.

Bogey Margaret, go do what you're doing. Lee will have rice.

Lee Potatoes in grease cripples me stomach.

Lauren He's hit the nail on the head. Potatoes – swimming in grease.

Bogey I'm telling you for the last time.

Lauren There's a few last times going on round here.

Bogey *drags* **Lauren** *up off his chair and pushes her towards the hallway.*

Lauren *goes upstairs.*

Margaret *takes the whiskey and two glasses from the drop-leaf table's cupboard.*

Lee   Just let me give them a little rinse.

Margaret *follows him into the kitchen.*

Margaret   The tea towel's where it usually is.

Lee   The immersion's fixed?

Margaret   Sixteen pounds and he won't give me a penny towards it.

Lee   Running hot water's a real luxury.

Bogey *gets settled in his chair in the living room.*

Bogey   Them arrive on the island yet?

Peter   Just now.

Bogey   I'd cling on to her meself.

Peter *stares at his dad.*

Bogey   Tell me you wouldn't.

Peter   She screams too much.

Bogey   So them all stay. Drink the Babycham I bought for yous.

Peter   I'm all right with the ginger beer.

Bogey   Ginger and a little whiskey.

Peter   It makes me sick.

Bogey   It's good for you, man. Little, little keeps the cold out.

Peter   I'm all right with this, Dad, honest.

Bogey   Don't ever let anyone push you, you hear, into nothing you don't want.

In the kitchen, **Margaret** *takes the glass that* **Lee** *has been rinsing the life out of and dries it on the tea towel.*

Margaret   Not bad news, is it?

Lee   No news at all, missus.

Margaret   From back home? From his family?

Lee   There's nothing affecting him.

Margaret   An earthquake wouldn't move that fucker.

Lee   He doesn't like fuss is all.

Margaret   You'd tell me if there was anything?

Lee   Bogey will tell you if he wants you to know.

He takes the glasses and goes into the living room.

Break out the ginger wine and we'll make two whiskey macs.

Margaret *comes in, the tea towel still in her hand, and takes another glass from the drop-leaf table's cupboard.*

Margaret   I thought you were watching the film.

Peter   Can I go out, Dad?

Bogey   One's all she's having.

Margaret   One's all I want for now.

Lee *pours him and* **Bogey** *two healthy measures.* **Margaret** *forces him to fill her glass.*

Lee   To the Lord and His Son.

Margaret   And all the other poor bastards born on this Earth.

Lee   Amen.

Peter   I'll come back for me dinner.

Margaret   You're not wandering the streets, today of all days, like you've no home to go to.

Lee   You don't want ginger?

Margaret   If something's strong you leave it. You can't do nothing if it's weak already.

Bogey Turn up the telly, Peter. This is the bit where he takes her prisoner.

Margaret You wish.

Bogey There ain't a hand big enough for Miss Margaret.

Margaret You got something right.

Lee I'll just have a little, like so, of the white meat. The rice is no problem as long as it's washed good. All that starch.

Peter *and* **Bogey** *are watching* **Margaret** *guzzle her drink down.*

Bogey Watch your film, son. All monsters wind up with their arse chained eventually.

After staring at **Bogey**, **Margaret** *trounces off to the kitchen.*

She pours herself another glass of Guinness but doesn't hide the bottle this time.

She gets the sprouts ready and puts them on to boil.

Bogey, **Lee** *and* **Peter** *relax in front of the TV.*

Bogey *nods off again.*

Lee It's bad, man, when he's up the building. Not as bad as *Mighty Joe* though. And *Frankenstein*, Lord God. Him and the blind pickney. I can't watch it.

Peter You seen *Ben* yet?

Lee I don't like them modern. All colour in your face.

Peter Nah, Lee, *Ben*'s real sad. This boy and his rat.

Lee Rat. Them a make film about rat now?

Margaret (*in the kitchen doorway*) This'll be ten minutes, no more.

Lee You hear this, Margaret? Them a make film about rat now.

Margaret Crying his bloody eyes out.

Peter   I wasn't.

Margaret   All right, you wasn't. Pull the table out.

Peter   He's just got to New York.

Margaret   I don't give a fuck where he is. Pull the table out. And make sure the cloth's ironed.

Peter   I'm not ironing it.

Lee   There's no shame in being able to do for yourself.

Margaret   Go and give her a shout.

Lee   We were taught same as the girls. And if you didn't – bang – straight across your knuckles.

Margaret   He must have been half-dead then from his beatings. Look at him. There's no lazier fucker.

Lee   Mumma's favourite.

Margaret   Hey, King Farouk, your dinner's almost ready.

Lee   Leave him, Margaret. The man's in work all year.

Margaret   For who? You didn't hear me? Go up the stairs.

Peter   Fucking hell.

Margaret   Go up the stairs before I break your back in such a way they never fix it.

Lee   I'll pull the table out.

Margaret   One day a year I ask them to participate.

Peter *gets off the floor, goes to the door, and with his eyes still on the TV, calls:*

Peter   Lauren. Lauren. Lauren, you stupid bitch, you've gotta come down.

Bogey   What the raase is all the noise about?

Peter   Mum told me.

Bogey   Go up the fucking stairs and bring her down now.

Margaret   Talk to him like that again.

Peter   I'm going.

Lee   They're making films about rats now.

Bogey   You can't get a wink a sleep.

Lee   A thing you wouldn't kick.

Bogey   Six o'clock every morning – and me awake half the night, every night.

Lee   They should put my man *Frankenstein* on Or *Steptoe*, the man's nasty, you see.

Margaret *takes the tablecloth from the cupboard in the drop-leaf table. She shakes it out in front of the TV.*

Margaret   You wanna see that fool laughing at him.

Peter *comes back in.*

Peter   She's not hungry. Move that, Mam, I can't see the telly.

Margaret   She's not hungry. You hear that? She's not hungry. She's one bitch, that girl.

Lee   If she's not hungry – she's not hungry.

Margaret   I knew it the minute I clapped eyes on her . . .

Bogey   Go tell Lauren I said to come down.

Peter *stamps out of the room.*

Margaret   Not one. Not one good day outta a whole fucking year.

Bogey *kisses his teeth.*

Lee   This thing's only pulling so far.

Margaret *throws the tablecloth on the sofa.*

Margaret   Leave it.

Lee   I don't want to break it.

Margaret   Can't nobody else do nothing round here?

Bogey (*suddenly shouting towards the ceiling*)   Lauren, don't make me come up there.

Margaret   That's supposed to scare me, is it?

Bogey   You can't hush your noise for one day?

Peter *runs in.*

Peter   I brought the crackers, Mam.

He gets close to the TV to avoid the table.

Bogey   I've told you about your eyes already.

Lauren *comes in.*

Margaret (*throwing the tablecloth at her*)   Get this on the table. He's missed half his film cos of you.

Peter   This is a sad bit, Brother Lee.

Lee (*pouring another whiskey*)   I'll be with you in a minute.

Lauren, *despite herself, gets absorbed in setting three places at the table, going back and forth to the kitchen. To make the table look nice she divides the crackers between the three places and aligns the table mats in the centre. She fancy-folds the Christmas napkins.*

Margaret, *in the kitchen, puts the under-cooked roast potatoes in a dish. Drains the mushy sprouts into another. Sticks the cremated turkey on the platter. She puts two plates on a tray each. She puts rice on each of these plates.*

Lauren *comes in – she's searching the kitchen cupboard.*

Margaret   Tell him, the arse is burnt out of his rice.

Lauren   Is that what the smell is?

Margaret (*rubbing **Lauren**'s stomach*)   It breaks my heart to see you like this.

Bogey   Lauren, make sure and bring the pepper and the salt.

Margaret   Take the one he bought, or he'll have summat else to go on about.

Lauren   I can't find them candlesticks we bought. The ones with the holly on.

Margaret   The bastards melted the night your hair caught fire.

From living room.

Peter   Basil Brush.

Margaret   Take no notice of him, you have lovely hair.

Peter   That was brill though, wannit, Dad? The night her bush caught fire.

Margaret   People pay fortunes to have hair like yours.

Lee   Bastard miners – they should whip them, man, holding a whole country to ransom. Greed, you see . . .

Margaret *brings the two trays to the table.*

Margaret   Turn it over, and let's hear what the horse-faced German bitch has to say. A year older than me, she is only. That's what has the English the way they are – sucking up to every cunt.

Margaret *goes back for the two dishes of veg.*

Lauren *brings the turkey.*

Bogey *gets up.*

Margaret   Pete, you carve this year.

Peter *jumps up.*

Lauren *puts the turkey on the table and takes her place at the table.*

Bogey *waits behind* **Peter**.

Margaret *sits down.*

Lee *stays watching the film.*

Peter *hacks at the turkey.*

Bogey   Here, let me show you . . .

Bogey *does a few slices of breast, putting them on the tray plates first.*

Lauren   That smell's getting worse.

Bogey   You can't even cook a turkey.

Lauren *stands up to see what* **Bogey** *is pointing at.*

Lauren   The bag's melted all over the inside.

Bogey   You can't even cook a fucking turkey.

Margaret *stands up to investigate.*

Margaret   Where you sprang from they wouldn't know a fucking turkey if it jumped up and bit 'em. Bun and cheese. Bun and cheese on Christmas Day, if they're lucky.

Lee   The right cheese with the right bun.

Margaret   You wouldn't give a fuck what it was as long as it fits in your gullet.

Lee   Margaret, man, everybody makes mistakes.

Bogey   Not her, man. Not her.

Lee   It's the day of Our Lord.

Bogey   When everyone else will eat turkey.

Margaret   You want turkey, do yer?

Peter   Mam, don't.

Margaret   You want fucking turkey?

Lauren   Shut up, fool, she's not gonna stop now, is she?

Margaret   D'you want turkey I asked yer?

Bogey   Remember what happened last time.

Lee   Come here, son. Bogey, move the fucking turkey and stop pissing about.

Margaret   He has you all fooled. It's always me.

Lauren Well, shut up then, and let it be him if it's him.

Margaret Where he comes from they know no better. Brought up on a spit and a promise. They're all animals, Lauren. Irish, English, Indian, slant-eyed fuckers. They're all the same.

Lee (*coming to the table*) We can cut round it.

Lauren The whole turkey stinks of it.

Peter I'll eat it, Mam.

Margaret You cowardly little cunt.

Bogey The pickney know. The street know. And I'm to give you my money to keep the fucking twat in the off-licence.

Margaret *suddenly grabs the turkey and hurls it at him.*

Margaret See your turkey there.

Bogey *lunges for her.*

Lee *grabs him.* **Bogey** *doesn't struggle.* **Lee** *lets* **Bogey** *go.*

Bogey You carry on.

Margaret It should have broke your fucking jaw.

Bogey *is real quick. He grabs* **Margaret** *by the throat just as she reaches the kitchen door.* **Lee** *and* **Lauren** *reach* **Bogey** *just as he raises his fist.* **Margaret** *spits in* **Bogey**'s *face.*

Lee D'you wanna do life, man? Bogey. Bogey, hear me no. D'you wanna do life in this country? When you know how they stay already?

Bogey (*letting go*) I should have killed you years ago.

Margaret *runs into the kitchen. She grabs the bread knife from the cutlery drawer.*

Peter *runs in.*

Margaret (*swinging the bread knife*) Move outta me way.

Peter   Mam, stop now.

Lauren   She can't stop. You can't stop, can you, you fucking whore? Only a whore would have slept with a black man.

Margaret   I'm gonna kill him in here tonight. Move outta me way.

Peter   Mam, please.

Bogey   Kill me, come on, kill me if you're good.

Peter *runs and slams the door shut.* **Peter** *has his back to the door keeping it shut.*

Lee   It's the pickney I feel sorry for. Bad, you was bad back home, but you never hit woman.

Bogey   That thing's not a woman.

Margaret   And the chimp is? Move away from the door, you stupid little bastard, before I hurt you.

Peter   Dad, Dad, go out.

Bogey   I've run from me house for the last time.

Bogey *gets his machete out of the drop-leaf table's cupboard.*

Lauren   Fucking hell, Dad.

She runs to her side of the door and holds the handle to keep it pulled shut.

Lee   You're going too far this time.

Bogey   I've warned her – and I've warned her.

Peter   Lauren, make me dad go out.

Bogey   Peggy, I'm gonna kill you in here tonight.

Margaret   Still a fucking cannibal. Two fucking cannibals together – you'll make a lovely pair.

Bogey *chops into the door above* **Lauren***'s head.*

Lauren   Dad, she's not worth it.

Peter   Lauren, don't let the door go.

Margaret   An Irishman would have put his shoulder to it and had the whole house down by now.

Bogey *chops into the door again.*

Lee   I'm going for the police.

Lauren   Come and hold the door, you stupid black cunt.

Lee   This time, I'm going for the police. I'm warning you, Bogey. And make your father spin in him grave.

Peter   Mum, have a drink. Go on, get yourself a drink. Look, your Guinness is on the side.

Margaret   It's been there all week, son.

Bogey *chops into the door again.*

Peter   I know, Mum, just get a drink.

Lauren   Her and her fucking drink. You should have choked on your vomit. But you, you whinging bastard, had to call an ambulance. We'd be fucking rid of her now.

Bogey *smashes the machete into the door so it stays. He leaves it.*

Lee   He's put his down, Margaret.

Margaret   That bastard's given me a disease.

Bogey   Take no notice, missus.

He undoes his trousers and drops them to his knees to shows **Lauren** *a stain on the front of his long johns.*

Bogey   It's oil when I piss in work. My hands stain the front of them. Lee, lie me a tell?

Lee   From the metal. So my own stay.

Margaret   Four hours I spent in the special clinic.

Bogey (*doing up his pants*)   And her son stood right beside her. Man, you've no shame. Tell her, man. Tell her what you came here to tell me.

Margaret   Apart from filling his face.

Lee   It's all right – I know she's annoyed.

Margaret   Two week of penicillin. You don't believe me? Go in the drawer. Pete, go in the drawer. Look, I've put it down. Just go in the drawer. Go in the fucking drawer.

Lauren   He goes to work, comes home and sleeps in his chair. When's he supposed to meet these fucking women you're always on about?

Bogey   Leave it, you know how she stays.

Peter   There is pills, Lauren.

Bogey   You carry on and listen to her.

Margaret   They filleted me, cos I was riddled with his dirty diseases.

Bogey   Which thirteen-year-old womb's meant to bear pickney?

Margaret   Don't listen to him, Lauren.

Bogey   Seven years, she watched that man do. Rather than tell the truth.

Margaret   My nanna had enough shame to bear.

Peter (*giving* **Margaret** *the Guinness*)   Here, Mam.

Lauren *opens the kitchen door to stare at her mum.*

Margaret (*refusing the Guinness*)   It was Ireland, love. They'd never forgive yer.

Bogey   Here, see the money there. The two of you go to Kentucky. Make sure it's breast them give yer.

Lauren (*still looking at her mum*)   Kentucky's not fucking open today.

Lauren *turns away and starts cleaning the mess from the tipped-over table.* **Margaret** *comes out of the kitchen to help. They carry on until the floor is clean.*

Lauren   Find the replacement bulbs, Mam. Get the Mousetrap, Pete. We'll play upstairs.

Bogey   Let him watch the end of his film.

Peter   What'll we have now?

Margaret *rights the table.*

Margaret   We've got the ham. Pilchards will have to do you, Lee.

Lee (*to* **Peter** *about King Kong*)   Look at that eye. Imagine an eye like that a follow follow you.

Bogey   Peter, come here.

Peter *goes to his dad.* **Bogey** *lifts* **Peter**'s *face up by the chin.*

Peter   It's the film.

Lauren *leaves the room and goes upstairs.*

Margaret *takes the broken things into the kitchen.*

Lee   I can't bear it when they shoot him down.

Bogey (*to* **Peter**)   Go sit down.

Lee (*to* **Peter**)   Imagine that big fucker crashing down on your house, you'd soon fart.

Margaret *is leaning, head down against the kitchen table, getting her breath.* **Bogey** *goes in the kitchen and shuts the door.* **Margaret** *doesn't turn round.*

Bogey   Peggy – I'm fifty.

Margaret   You delight in goading me – you can't leave me when I'm peaceful.

Bogey   The pickney are grown up now.

Margaret   And who am I to find at this age, hey? Look at me.

Bogey   So I'm to chain my life for ever?

Margaret (*quiet*)   You're not leaving, Bogey.

Bogey (*grabbing her arm and making her look at him*)   You begged me to stay till Christmas – and Christmas it is.

Blackout.

Act Two

Evening.

The living room seems cold with just the males in and the overhead light on. They're watching True Grit *on the flickering TV.* **Bogey** *is sitting in his chair.* **Lee***, with his coat back on, is sitting closest to* **Bogey** *on the sofa.* **Peter** *is sitting on the other end of the sofa.*

The bedroom looks cosier, with the pink bedside lamp on. **Margaret** *is sitting on the edge of the bed, staring at* **Bogey***'s suitcase. Her reflection is caught in the full-length wardrobe mirror.*

After a while the bedroom door opens slowly. **Margaret** *doesn't look up.* **Lauren** *stares at her mum, staring at the suitcase.*

Lauren   D'you want me to make you a cup of tea?

No reply.

Lauren *goes to leave.*

Margaret   You finally managed it.

Lauren   What?

Margaret   You must be very proud.

Lauren   Of what exactly?

Margaret   From the hour you were born.

Lauren   Whatever.

She goes to leave again.

Margaret   You got what you wanted, girl.

Lauren   You don't want any tea, then?

Margaret   One clever, conniving, no-good little bitch.

Lauren   It takes one to know one.

Margaret   You wanna be careful I don't break your fucking neck.

Lauren   If he was going he'd have gone already.

Margaret   If I'd have had a gun that night I'd have shot you dead.

Lauren   Pity you didn't.

Margaret   Don't come fucking smart with me.

Lauren   Oh, fuck off.

She goes to leave.

Margaret   He goes – you go. You're fucking straight out that door. Believe me, lady. Hang out of his neck and tell him you love him – like you used – when you wanted ice cream. You're one sly little fucker.

Lauren   Did he send you, or did you come of your own accord this morning?

Margaret   Don't flatter yourself, love. He wanted his fourth pall-bearer back to cart him round on this throne. I've never wanted yer. Not from the hour you were born. Cry. No fucker on Earth cried like you. In the bed between us every fucking night. A grown man. A grown man lying in his bed a night a cry because of a whore like you.

Lauren   You showed me the ropes – you ugly old cunt.

Margaret   I'll show you something in a minute.

Lauren   You're not even able to stand.

Margaret *attempts to get up.*

Lauren   Come on if you're coming.

Margaret   When I get a hold of you.

Lauren   Everything's slipping through Margaret's fingers.

Margaret   One ungrateful bitch.

Lauren   Exactly what am I to be grateful for?

Margaret   You wait till I stand up.

Lauren I'm asking you a question. Hey. Think. Exactly what am I supposed to be grateful for?

Margaret *struggles to stand again.*

Lauren I asked you a question. I asked you a question. Look at the fucking state of yer. And I'm why he's leaving? He should have left years ago. He should have packed that years ago.

Margaret I gave up everything for you.

Lauren For him. Let's get it right. No one does it quite like blacks, do they, Mum? We know, don't we? The old fanny still twitching for black cock? From the big house straight to the slave quarters. Big Irish Margaret. All for the sake of a bit of black cock the wind howls outside and you can see the moon through the planks of your roof.

Margaret You've never liked me.

Lauren I love yer – you're me mam.

Margaret When I'm dead you'll be happy.

Lauren (*singing*)
      'Oh Danny Boy, the pipes the pipes are calling,
      From glen to glen . . .'

Come on – we not getting it tonight, are we not?

Margaret My nanna wouldn't speak to me.

Lauren The priest crossed the road. 'But you know I love you, Lauren. Me, you and Peter, we're our own little family.'

Margaret One cold, dead, fish-eyed bitch – just like the other fella downstairs.

Lauren D'you want tea or don't yer?

Margaret Get me the other bottle.

Lauren You've ate nothing all day.

Margaret I'd take nothing off the likes of you.

Lauren   Sit up properly.

Pause.

Margaret   I wouldn't be no more than five minutes in the Bowling Green and he'd be in behind me. A whole month it took him to come up and talk. The minute he touched me, Lauren.

Pause.

Don't you like the moon when it's that colour? Once, when we came out, and it was big at the end of the street, massive, like a great ball, as if it had fell out of the sky. You know that stupid bastard. You know how fucking backward he can be, he only thought it was the end of the world.

Lauren   You're gonna come off the bed.

Margaret   The way you stand, hold your head – both of you favour him. Never another for either of us from that day to this.

Lauren   You're gonna wind up on the floor.

Margaret   Look at the state of me. These fucking veins on me legs. No wonder he doesn't business with me.

Lauren *sits on the bed beside her mum. Both stare into the mirror at themselves and the case.*

Lauren   You can diet. And why the fuck you pay 'em to do that to your hair is beyond me.

Living room.

Bogey   Go see how much rice there, in the pan.

Peter *doesn't react quickly enough.*

Bogey   Don't make me ask you again.

Peter *gets up and goes to the kitchen door. He turns the strip lighting on and waits for it to light before he'll go into the cleaned, stark kitchen. He takes the pan off the stove and comes to the kitchen door to show his dad.*

Bogey   Leave the light on.

Bogey *gets the whiskey out washes his head. Warms his jumper and extra socks again ready to go in the kitchen. He gets up and goes to the kitchen, taking the pan off* **Peter** *as he goes through the door.*

Lee   Fry the rice in a little oil and onion for the three a we. No bodder give me pilchards – me can't stomach nothing with entrails.

Bogey *snatches the onions from the veg rack and the chopping board from behind the taps and starts to cut the onions.*

Peter   I don't like rice, Dad.

Bogey (*roars*)   How many pickney in the world a starve? Time you woke up to raase.

Bedroom.

Lauren   If he was going he'd have gone already. Who'll clean his boots and run his bath? They don't even have running water. Him digging yam and killing chickens – you're joking, aren't yer? He'd starve before he'd cook. It takes him all his time to get out the fucking chair.

Margaret   What will I do, Lauren?

Lauren   Play it cool. When he gets no response he'll soon –

Margaret   I'll wipe me arse on every stitch before I'll let it leave here.

Lauren   If we sit up here quiet I guarantee he'll be up sooner or later.

Margaret   He used to love you, Lauren. He really loved you.

Lauren   I know.

Living room.

Bogey (*from kitchen*)   Raase hole.

Lee   What do you, sah?

Bogey (*from kitchen*)   Nearly take the top off me fucking finger to raase.

Lee   Come and sit down – I'll do it.

Bogey (*from kitchen*)   Me nah invalid.

Peter   Run it under the cold tap.

Lee (*on his way to the kitchen*)   The pickney have more sense. Give me the knife here.

Lee *takes off his coat and hangs it on the back of the kitchen door. Rolls up his sleeves. Takes off his cap and bangs it for dust on his thigh plenty of times before putting it back on. He starts to cut the onions on the Formica table.*

Bogey   Use the chopping board – you want her kick off altogether?

Peter *turns the TV up. There is pure gun fights on.*

Lee   Is them cut the dog.

Bogey   Move outta me way.

Bogey *gets the tea towel and bandages his hand.*

Lee   I'd only like to get me hands on them.

Bogey   And do what, old man?

Lee   You go carry on till your head bursts, that's all I can say. Each day hang on you like a John Crow but still you want struggle. Your mind can't make up this way or that.

Bogey   Turn the telly down before I come in there you see.

Peter *turns the TV down.*

Lee   What me tell you say from morning? What me tell you say? But you're there, don't want listen. But you'll listen when it's too late. Then you'll listen once too often.

Bogey   Go long home.

Lee   Home me want go – go eat some proper food.

Bogey   Go home then.

Lee   It's the pickney I feel sorry for.

Bogey   Cut the raase-hole onion if you're cutting it.

Lee *cuts the onion.*

Lee   A make house on sand. – while you and she ride towards each other. Champions. Champions to raase. A fly flag. A fly banner. But when it comes to night-time you fluff the same cushion in the same tent.

Bogey *wraps his finger tighter.*

Lee   If you want rut with the woman, rut. At least then the pickney know where them stand. Them don't know them head from them arse. But that don't have to concern you. Don't have to concern Mr Big Man. As long as him have her pinned by her throat he's happy. Nah so it go, Bogey? You answer me that Nah so it go?

Bogey *carries on tightening the tea-towel bandage.*

Lee   Keep tightening it – that might go numb too.

Bogey   Me a go sit down.

Lee   Do as you like – you always do.

Bogey *goes into the living room.* **Peter** *stares at his hand.*

Bogey   It's all right. Sit where you're there. It's all right, me say.

Peter *turns back to the TV.*

Bedroom.

Margaret   The day after you came back in the state you are now, the Hartnetts bought the shop on Claremont Road. Oh, she made sure to tell him in full view of everyone in the porkshop. I'd have give her one look, you see. Her and the two mealy-mouthed fuckers she calls daughters. 'You'd have a hard job finding anyone to fuck either of them.' That's what I'd have told her.

Lauren   I went to the spiritualist church yesterday.

Margaret   You don't want to be messing with them things. How long have we been up here?

Lauren   Mum.

Margaret   It's over. The best thing for it.

Lauren   It's different when it's you, though. When it's you the world has to come to a fucking standstill. You and fucking him. It's not fucking over, you idiot. When this thing's born I'll have to look at it for the rest of me life.

Margaret   D'you wanna end up like me? Is that what you want? Is this how you wanna end up? Listen to me now and listen good. He was a no-good fucker. Out for himself.

Lauren   And the thing downstairs is any better?

Margaret   He goes to work.

Lauren   To pay the mortgage on his castle that you've no stake in. And when he's ready, which seems sooner than later, he'll sell up and live life like a king where he came from with his chimp as queen.

Margaret   Once they've ridden the mule, Lauren, the mule goes back in the stable. They don't give a fuck any of 'em. You've had your brush with it, be glad it's over. It only burns so long for them, Lauren. Be thankful it ended in full flow.

Lauren   Let him go then.

Margaret   Dead is easy. One blanket. One grey blanket when I met him first. All of this we did together. From one room to this. Nine hundred pounds we paid for this, Lauren. Whether he holds the deeds or not, I've contributed. Every stitch of furniture. Every meal down his throat. Every postal order to the five bastards over there belong to him. I'll watch him burn in hell first before I let that big-arsed bitch benefit from anything we've achieved.

Lauren   I was the last to see him before the ventilator.

Margaret Come here.

Lauren *won't go.*

Living room.

Lee (*in kitchen doorway*) You want your pilchards warmed up in a pan or fried with your rice?

Bogey I don't give a raase-hole what you do with it.

Lee A simple question me ask. A simple answer it needs – no more.

Bogey A hang round people's lives.

Lee One day you go thank me. A prison cell me a save you from. Either that or madness.

Bogey Madness no take me long time. Years ago. Straight here. Here in me chest. How I can't talk. Can't sleep. Me shoulders a hot me. Me back a hot me. Me legs don't work like them used. I can barely walk.

Lee Vain, you're vain, since morning. Proud and vain.

Bogey Me no ask you chat more foolishness. You want stand round and listen, well, open your ears and shut your mouth. No bodder leave, Peter. I'm beyond shouting and carrying on. Them days done. All me a do is wait out my time. Neither you nor your sister me have problem with. But you see that woman. Sooner the devil take me. Me and you don't talk. Me and me own pickney don't even know each other. You see how that pains me. Me and that girl upstairs . . .

Quiet.

Go tell her there's food here if she wants it.

Peter You know how she'll be if I go up.

Bogey She's still your mumma. She won't want any. Call your sister from the door and come straight back. If *she* stops you, you tell her I said you must come.

Peter   That'll only make her worse.

Lee   I'll shout her.

Bogey   And have Miss Lion kick off altogether? I go call her meself.

Peter   I'll shout her from the top of the landing.

Peter *leaves the room.*

Lee   You want me fry it or not?

Bogey   With any luck it'll stick in me throat and kill me.

Lee   It's true for the woman, them a go give you award yet.

He suddenly slams down the spatula and comes to the doorway.

Go up the stairs, unpack the suitcase in front of her and let her see where you stand for once. I can't see what it a go cost you.

No response.

Bull-headed from morning.

Peter (*at the top of the stairs*)   Lauren, there's dinner down here if you want it.

Bedroom.

Margaret (*shouting to him*)   Come here, you.

Peter   There's dinner downstairs, me dad said.

Margaret   Don't tell me he's got off his lazy arse.

Peter   Me dad said, Lauren.

Margaret   Come here, you little weasel.

Peter *runs back down.*

Margaret (*shouting after him*)   I was only gonna give you the Quality Street. Lauren, pass me the Quality Street.

Lauren *opens* **Margaret***'s side of the wardrobe which is full of* **Margaret***'s cloths. She gets the Quality Street.*

Lauren   He'll know you're only gone down to see him.

Margaret *undoes the Quality Street.*

Margaret   Take what you want.

Lauren   I can't eat chocolate either.

Margaret *throws the sweets on the floor and stamps them into the rug.*

Margaret   Slimy little fucker. Growing up the wrong way already.

Lauren   How's that benefited yer?

Margaret   Saves some other poor fucker's daughter putting up with the cheek of him. I'll show 'em all before I'm finished.

Living room.

Bogey   She coming?

Peter   Dunno.

Bogey   No, the other one's too busy filling her head full a shit.

In the kitchen, **Lee** *puts the food on four plates. He puts one in the oven. He takes* **Peter** *and* **Bogey** *their food.*

Peter *puts his on the table and goes for the knives and forks and salt and pepper.* **Peter** *has his back to the fire.* **Lee** *comes back with his plate.* **Bogey** *drags the table towards himself.* **Lee** *has to pull his chair towards the table to use it.*

Bogey (*to* **Peter**)   Go sit the other side – you want dry up your lungs?

Peter *slides his plate across.*

Lee   Move up a little, let me see my man finish the fucker. So twist foot walk, you know. One redskin man. Same way as my man there.

Bogey   You can't hear what the man a say?

Peter   I have moved.

Bogey   You call that move? Move up, me say.

Gunshots on the TV.

Peter   Don't take it out on me.

Lee   Almost thirteen years it's took – finally him talk. Eat your food, son, while it's still there on your plate. You never know when them a go open fire. We might need our strength to cart one a them a hospital.

Bogey *kisses his teeth.*

Lee *gets up and takes some crackers from beside the tree.*

Lee   Take no notice a him – he's been miserable since the hour he was born. You know your mumma's trouble? Him have one drink too many the night they met and him smile by mistake.

Bogey   You stand there and laugh.

Lee   What else you expect me fi do?

Lee *coaxes* **Peter** *to pull the cracker.*

Bedroom.

Margaret   What the fuck are they doing?

Living room.

Lee *puts the Christmas hat on top of his cap.*

Lee   Me can't afford to catch head cold at my age.

Bedroom.

Lauren   We'll never see a Christmas together.

Living room.

Lee *and* **Peter** *pull another cracker.*

Bedroom.

Margaret   What the fuck are they doing?

Living room.

Lee (*shooting* **Peter** *with the tiny plastic gun out of the cracker*)
Get off your horse and nam your milk.

Lee *puts the new hat on* **Peter**'s *head and picks up another cracker.*

Bogey   You carry on and when she's stood there beside you
you'll soon fart.

Peter   You just don't want to wear the hat, d'yer?

Lee   The boy's waking up at last.

Bedroom.

Margaret   I'll pull his fucking innards out.

Lauren   As if me dad'll be pulling crackers. And if he is
he's only doing it to do this to yer. If you go down you'll
have lost. For once, Mam, be the stronger one.

Margaret   I could murder a drink.

Lauren   You'll be all right.

Margaret   Tea – anything.

Lauren   Anyway, you go down them stairs you've lost.
He'll be sweating just like you. Understand that. If you learn
to understand that things'll be better in the future. He won't
be able to fuck with you all the time.

Lauren *picks up the hairbrush as she turns the radio on. Christmas
carols come on.*

Margaret   Turn that shit off.

Lauren *finds a soothing Andy Williams-playing channel. Sitting on
the floor in front of the bed, she holds up the brush.*

Lauren   Come on. Then I'll do yours like we used.

Eventually **Margaret** *sits on the bed behind* **Lauren** *and brushes her hair.*

Living room.

Bogey   Save some for the other two.

Lee   Twelve in a box, sah. One of them little parachute man me a look for.

Bogey *lifts his plate and pushes the table away. He eats off his lap.*

Lee   What you buy me this year, sah? What you buy your big brother?

Peter   He never buys nobody nothing.

Bogey   What you call that? (*Re untouched bike.*) You know how much it cost me?

Peter   If she'd have been here it'd have been the fucking fiver.

Bogey   Five pounds to you is nothing?

Lee   Leave it now.

Peter *pushes his uneaten plate of rice across the table.*

Bogey   Pick up your knife.

Peter   You fucking pick it up.

Bogey's *quick out of his chair. He has* **Peter** *by the arm.*

Bogey   You think me a go watch you go the same way as the other one? You think so? I'll see you dead first. Go sit down. If I see one grain. Just one grain.

Lee   Rather than sit the pickney down and talk to him.

Bogey   You want me talk to him?

Lee   Like any woman. Any bitch. No wonder the woman drinks.

Bogey   What me can't understand is why you don't have the courage to take her. See her there. Take her. You want her – take her. You must think, fool, I'm fool, all these years. Stand up and take her if you good.

Lee *takes his plate to the kitchen.*

Bogey   Yes, Lee. No amount of snivelling at the woman's heels can resurrect it if it don't live. If it don't live it don't live – you understand me.

Lee *comes out of the kitchen with his coat.*

Bogey   You nah finish your food. Miss Margaret's hands don't make it – so it don't sweet. You don't even see what time has done to them. But they say it's blind all the same. You want me send him go tell Miss Margaret you want her. That's right, make like you can't hear. The spoils, man. It's already spoilt. Like a mango months from a tree. It's mash up beyond recognition. When you get lucky and lift her skirt, you'll see. Just give me time enough to leave this fucking country.

He picks up his plate and goes into the kitchen.

Lee   When – in the whole of creation?

Bedroom.

'God Didn't Make Little Green Apples' is on the radio in the bedroom.

Margaret   Remember you used love this twat. The only knickers I'd be throwing'd have half-bricks in 'em.

Lauren   You should see a psychiatrist, Mam. They're good. They make you see things about yourself.

From the top drawer of the bedside cabinet **Margaret** *takes out an old pair of* **Lauren**'s *pink plastic bobbles for the plaits she's given her.*

Margaret   If you're stupid enough to do shit like that. Hold still.

Lauren   Dr Colville said it was good you and him didn't visit.

Margaret   There's not one of them worth taking your life for. Dead or alive.

Lauren   Let me brush all that lacquer out of yours now.

They swap places.

Living room.

Bogey   She was cheap, man. One bottle a whiskey. (*Taking a fresh bottle out of the cupboard.*) Every night for a week. But you're too cheap to pay that. Your mumma I'm talking, Peter.

Lee   What you a tell the boy for?

Bogey   Miss Lion of the backstreet pub. What them call it? Where she used sit in a corner with her so-called husband. One half-pint a pale ale each as she watched him drink his dole money cos him can't find work for his wort'less raase. One week a whiskey me feed him till him eye-blind to what she was carrying on with. One week for her to leave his table and lie down in my bed.

Bogey *pours three glasses of whiskey.*

Lee   Peter, go up the stairs.

Bogey   Four pickney she leave when she was pregnant with your sister. You never knew that. Four innocent pickney.

Lee   And you never knew before you enticed the woman.

Bogey   Romp me a look for. Romp.

Peter   You dirty old cunt.

Lee   Lie him a tell. Living eye water him cry from the hour him step from the ship. Set sail like lion and lay down in this country like dog. Him one a go conquer a fortune. Him couldn't even step outside if me nah walk beside him. Only the love a that woman stop him from cry. Nah, so it go, Bogey?

Bogey   Yes, me a cunt. But me pay, man. Me pay with me life. Look pon the barbed wire shot through every part a me body.

Bedroom.

Lauren *has brushed her mum's hair out of the set. It's still frizzy but* **Lauren** *has managed to force a 1950s curl in the bottom.*
Lauren *goes to the wardrobe. She pulls out the only thing hanging in a plastic dust cover.*

Lauren (*unzipping it*)   Stand up.

Margaret   Leave me alone.

Lauren   Stand up.

Margaret   Stop pissing about.

Lauren   Mam, just stand up.

Margaret   I will in me arse.

Lauren   You wanna keep him? (*Pause.*) Stand up then.

Margaret *stands up.*

Lauren *pulls out the well-cut, sleeveless, round-necked, black jazz-singer-type dress.*

Lauren   Longer things give you a better shape.

Margaret   That's for funerals. With the long jacket to cover the tops of me arms.

Lauren   It'll hide the marks on your legs. Put it on. Let me get me bag.

Lauren *leaves the room.*

Margaret *takes her crimplene skirt, her acrylic cardigan and her slip off. She gets her long-line foundation garment out of the bedside cabinet and puts it on over her roll-on-type girdle. She undoes her surgical stockings from the girdle, then struggles to pull it from underneath the foundation garment. When the girdle's at her feet she attaches her surgical stockings to the foundation garment.*

Living room.

Bogey *switches the TV off. He offers a glass of whiskey to* **Peter**.

Bogey   Take it.

Peter   No.

Lee   Take it, man.

Peter   No.

Lee   I don't give a fuck, man, just give me the drink.

Bogey   We come from a respectable family. We grandpappy was a white man. Long silver hair to so. Lie me a tell, Lee. Father a constable. A big dark chap – wouldn't fit through that door. Live on our own plot a land atop Lawrence Hill. Cousins all around. Can step from our yard and look out across whole heap a tree in every direction. The Blue Mountains.

Pause.

Bedroom.

Lauren *enters her mother's bedroom just as* **Margaret** *has finished changing her girdle.*

Lauren   Sit on the bed.

She takes a series of creams from her bag.

Condition, tone and moisturise first. Take your glasses off.

Margaret *sits on the edge of the bed looking up as* **Lauren** *pours the first of her mixtures on to her pink cotton-wool ball and starts rubbing at* **Margaret***'s face.*

Living room.

Bogey   From when say her grandmother told the lie that mash up the man's life – she couldn't be right. Bad blood runs through you like rock. Her mumma had four different pickney for four different men in 1920. Not today. Not how it stand today in 1974. In Ireland in 1920. Your mumma lay down and let man breed her up at thirteen. One white woman that. She left her kids and never look back. To this day me have yet to meet one of them. And now your sister. Could a been a doctor, a lawyer, a whole manner a things –

how them love pin her with prize. Upstairs a breed pickney to a dead field nigger me couldn't even look pon. A thing you wouldn't kick. As sure as the moon follows the sun it a go follow you.

Pause.

Bedroom.

Lauren You should moisturise regularly. You should look after yourself.

Margaret And who's to provide the money and the time?

Lauren Green's better on older women.

Margaret You'll have me looking half a fool.

Lauren Just sit still, it fucking kills if you get it in your eye.

Margaret I'm too old for this, Lauren.

Lauren Look, that eye looks better than this already and when we get the mascara on –

Margaret I'll look like a whoor altogether.

Living room.

Bogey You must careful where you plant your seed. You hear me? No make your whatsit cage you. So many minutes a pleasure a whole lifetime waste.

*He gets up and starts fiddling with the Christmas tree lights. When they won't come on he goes to the kitchen for his toolbox from under the sink. He has to remove **Margaret**'s Guinness bottles to reach it.*

Bedroom.

Lauren See, you look great. Put the dress on now.

Margaret I'll feel a fool.

Lauren You'll look great.

Margaret   He'll laugh after me.

Lauren   Mum, you love each other – when are you gonna understand that?

Lauren *helps* **Margaret** *into the dress.* (*It fitted* **Margaret** *in another time.*)

Bogey *comes back to the living room with his toolbox and starts fiddling with the Christmas tree lights.*

'Love Letters' by Ketty Lester comes on the radio in the bedroom.
Margaret *out-sings it.* **Lauren** *is on her hands and knees pulling a weighty hat box from the bottom of* **Margaret***'s side of the wardrobe.*

Lauren (*pulling 1950s black peep-toe high heels from the box*)   All those years I waited and me feet got too big.

Margaret   We polished many a dance floor wearing these. Knife-straight seams up the backs of sheer black stockings.

Lauren (*pulling out 1950s costume jewellery*)   You haven't destroyed the square quartz set he bought you the week he did nights?

Margaret (*dancing*)   In their case in the bottom under the photograph of the kids.

Margaret *sweeps up* **Lauren** *to dance with her to 'Love Letters'. When it ends* **Lauren** *roots out the costume jewellery.*

Living room.

Peter   I'll go back to school proper, Poppa.

Bogey *carries on fiddling with the lights.*

Peter   They give you classes to catch up.

Bogey   No bodder your head, sah.

The tree lights come on. **Lee** *puts the TV on. It's Tommy Cooper.*
Bedroom.

Lauren   Just the earrings and the necklace; the brooch will be a bit much. Put 'em in yourself. I can't stomach putting 'em in other people's ears.

Margaret   Watch the clasp on the back of me dress, it cost an arm and a leg fifteen years ago.

Living room.

Bogey *takes his toolbox back to the kitchen. He puts the Guinness bottles back in place in front of the toolbox.*

Bedroom.

Lauren (*re red lipstick*)   Go like this with the tissue.

Margaret   You're teaching your mother to suck eggs.

Lauren   You look like a jazz singer.

Margaret   Every fucker can stop wondering what the fuck happened to Baby Jane you mean. I look like an old trollop. Look at this. If I flap hard enough I can fly down and shit on him.

Lauren   You've not looked this good in years.

Margaret   I bet these don't fit no more either – not with the way me feet swell up.

Back in the living room **Bogey** *slams the kitchen door to make sure it is shut.*

Margaret   You hear the door?

Bogey *wedges an old blanket behind the living-room door as a draught excluder. He turns the fire full on before settling down in his chair.*

Margaret   You hear the door downstairs?

She snatches her glasses on.

You heard the door slam? As plain as day.

Lauren   Let him come up if he's coming up.

Margaret   So I won't hear him open the back one.

Lauren   Mum, I guarantee you it's a fucking game.

She bars the door.

Margaret   What the fuck's he playing at?

Lauren   Don't even answer.

Margaret   Move out the way of the door.

Lauren *won't move.*

Margaret   Move out the way of the door.

Lauren *won't move.*

Margaret   Don't let me tell you again. Stand back from the door.

Lauren *won't move.*

Margaret   Move out the way of the door – I can't put it any plainer.

Lauren   For once in your life you're gonna have some fucking dignity.

During the tussle, **Lauren** *knocks* **Margaret***'s glasses off.* **Margaret** *grabs* **Lauren***'s plait. Still holding it,* **Margaret** *bends to pick her glasses up.*

Margaret   I used walk down O'Connell Street – head held high. The best legs. A waist you could put your hands around. They all wanted me, Lauren. All of them. Even the manager of O'Reilly's. Wouldn't even look back when they'd whistle. And they would. They were all jealous. All the scrawny bitches back home. Me hair. Me looks. Me nanna used to say – sure the very air we breathe wasn't good enough for that woman – 'She's not for marrying.' I come from a good family, Lauren. A step-up from the likes of them. They can't even read or write. And to think I slept with that – that from the gutter – that thing from a mud hut.

Standing, **Margaret** *throws the glasses on the bed.*

Margaret   You wanna walk in these shoes? I'd kill that fucker first before I'd take me own life. That's the difference between me and you, Lauren.

Lauren   There's nothing worse than an Irish bitch on heat.

Margaret   So much for your meditation and love-'em beads.

Margaret *leaves the bedroom.*

Lauren *is sitting on the floor, her back to the door.*

Living room.

Bogey *is staring at the card on his unopened present off* **Lauren.**

Lee *is sitting on the arm of the sofa facing the door.*

The living room door smashes open.

Margaret   Yes – I had a baby at thirteen. The bastard pushed me down in a field. My so-called brother ran off.

In the bedroom, **Lauren**'s *waters break.*

Margaret   Five it was when it died – twisted like hazel wood – never walked a day in its life.

Lauren *takes her knickers off to mop the floor.*

Margaret   Hear Sister breeda now, as I'm stood over his little white coffin – cos you can't stay at home, only the nuns are charitable enough. 'That's God's punishment for making yourself available.'

Lauren's *in pain.*

Lauren   Danny. Danny, are you there?

Margaret   You held me close – didn't yer, fucker – the first time you heard that tale.

Margaret *snatches the present from* **Bogey**'s *hand.*

Margaret   It says from the sly fucker – all my love.

Bogey (*to* **Peter**)   Go get me hat.

Margaret *takes* **Bogey**'s *whiskey from the cupboard, opens the cap and drinks straight from the bottle.*

Margaret   Bogey in his flat cap for work and his dapper little trilby to go gallivanting, Bogey the English gentleman.

To them you'll always be black, a spade, a coon. Don't you
get it?

Bogey   Go get me hat.

Lee   You can't leave them, man.

Bogey   She's one of them, man. They won't trouble her.

Margaret   Sit down, half-breed. They're neither donkey
nor horse. My own sisters couldn't look at 'em.

Bogey   Go get me hat.

Still holding the whiskey, **Margaret** *rips open the present from*
Lauren*.*

Margaret   Your little half-breed's choose you a blinder
here. White, hey, Lauren – just like the man I met. You
used look something in your white shirts. Didn't you, boyo?
All open-necked and pressed to buggery. But you were still
black. You'll always be black. Going back to the chimp, are
we? This whole day's misery orchestrated for that.

Lauren *is on all fours in pain.*

Margaret (*to* **Lee**)   What time did she put in her note,
Judas?

Bogey   You wanna see the message he came give me, you
crazy bitch?

Bogey*'s suddenly out of his chair. He has* **Margaret***, still holding
the whiskey, by the back of her neck, dragging her through the house
into the street. He drags her in front of the writing on their wall.*

Lee (*to* **Peter**)   Sit down and watch your telly.

Margaret   Who wrote that on our wall? (*Screaming.*) Which
one of you bastards wrote that?

Bogey *runs and shelters in their doorway throughout.*

Lauren (*screams*)   Mam!

Peter *jumps up, pushes the bike over, runs into the unlit kitchen and
slams the door.*

Lee (*picking up the bike*)   It don't rain but it pours.

He goes into the hallway.

Margaret *is still in the street, screaming at the neighbours.*

Margaret   Yes – what's in the cat is *surely* in the kitten. That's right, bastards – hide. You think I can't see yer with your stiff little lives. You wouldn't know living if it jumped up and bit yer.

A light comes on in one of the neighbour's bedrooms.

Margaret   You cowardly cunts. Yes, I'm the sinner who pays your passage to heaven – for as sure as hell there's nothing in the balance either way.

Bogey (*gritted teeth*)   Get your backside in here now.

Margaret   Come and get me. No – you wouldn't do that. Too fucking scared of what this lot will think. Bogey whose nose is browner than it need be. Bogey who makes every excuse for the fact that he's even fucking alive. They're no better. They're no fucking better than me or you.

Bogey   If I come out there you see.

Margaret   You don't get it, do yer? Tell them good morning. Tip your hat. Beg them a gentlemanly good night. They'll never forgive yer. (*Answering the new light that has come on in another neighbour's bedroom. Lifting up her dress.*) This is what he sees in me. Which is more than can be said for any of you dried-up old bitches. (*Reply.*) Yes, I'm bloody disgusting. He's there. D'you want him? Shall I whistle him for yer? The little smiley-faced piccaninny. He's just in the doorway. Bogey. You love that, don't you? Humphrey. His fucking name's Humphrey. Come on, Humphrey Rudolph Leonard Lawrence, show them your true colours – drag me in, why don't you?

Bogey   Come in now.

Margaret (*addressing new light in a new window*)   Well, you two-faced old whoor, don't think I haven't seen you hanging out of the thing you call a dress for this thing's benefit. There's nothing worse than an Irish bitch on heat.

Bogey   Peggy.

Margaret   These are the kind, these you perform for, wouldn't even lend me a matinee coat for her in St Mary's until you could call from work. These. These lot. Come on down. One of you, I dare you. Come on out. Cos as sure as I stand here today – I'll do time. You wanna look down your nose at me. I'D DO IT ALL AGAIN. D'you hear me? There's not one fucking thing in my life I'm ashamed of. Put all the signs in the windows you like and when I'm ready . . . You see that brick. You see that half a brick. And when the ambulance comes to cart you away I'll stab that fucker too. You've pushed me too far once too fucking often. Judge me till there's not a breath left in this body? You've another thing coming. Every last one of yer.

Silence for a while.

She suddenly sits down in the middle of the street.

Silence for a while.

Look at us, Bogey. Look at us.

Bogey   Come. Come, Margaret.

Margaret   We've made such a mess of it all.

Silence for a while.

She breaks the whiskey bottle on the pavement. She drunkenly slashes at her wrist.

Bogey   You nah cut bad. Stand up. Stand up, Margaret. No bodder let them stare pon you.

Margaret   Leave me.

Bogey   Me know.

Margaret   My mother wouldn't write to me.

Bogey   Stand up now and come in the house. (*Shouting to the upstairs of their house.*) Lauren, bring a tea towel, come give me.

No reply.

Bogey (*shouting*)   You no hear me? Bring cloth come give me.

Margaret   No child added that to the wall.

Bogey   You're hardly bleeding. Get up. Get to your feet.

Lauren   MAM – HELP ME!

Lee *goes upstairs.*

Bogey   You can't hear your pickney a call? Stand up. (*Pause.*) While my heart still open.

The lights in the street's bedroom windows are gradually going out.

Lee *enters the bedroom, twisting his stained white hanky into a knot.*

Lee   Same place your mumma crouch to have your brother. You're all right. Bite on this when your pain comes. Whole heap a hog me deliver back home – while your fool father quiver in a stupor like him do about everything.

Lauren   Hedging your bets, hey, Lee?

Lee   Take it. Me nah use it yet.

Lauren   So you never have to buy your own whiskey.

Lee   Take it, missus.

Lauren   Stick it up your arse.

Bogey   Me a go in, Peggy.

Lauren *goes down the stairs.* **Lee** *follows her down.* **Lauren** *gets her coat.*

Bogey (*to* **Lauren**)   Where you a go?

Lauren   The night you threw me out I was frightened. But not as much as I am being back here.

Pause.

Bogey   Me a go in, missus, it's up to you where you go.

Lauren *goes outside.*

Margaret   Lauren.

Lauren   I don't belong here no more.

Margaret   Don't be stupid.

Bogey   Lee, shut the door.

Bogey *goes in the living room. He pours himself a glass of white rum.*

Lauren   Go on in. (*Pause.*) He's gonna shut the door.
(*Pause.*) If I stay out overnight I lose my room.

Margaret   Stay there.

Margaret *goes in to* **Peter** *in the kitchen.* **Lee** *watches* **Lauren** *at the door.*

Margaret   Take the bike and ride with her to the bus stop.

Bogey   The bike stays where it is.

Lee *shuts the front door and enters the living room.*

Bogey *pours three more glasses of white rum. He leaves one on top of the drop-leaf table.*

Bogey   White rum.

Lee   Thank you, sah.

Bogey   See it there, Margaret, you take it when you're
ready. Take the glass, boy.

Peter *refuses the rum.* **Margaret** *leaves the room.*

Bogey   It will still be there when you come back.

Margaret *gets her coat on the way to the front door.* **Lauren** *is gone.*

Lee   Merry Christmas.

Bogey   Turn the telly up.

Lee   Me raase – *Bridge on the River Kwai.*

Margaret *shuts the front door. She goes upstairs and sits on the end of the double bed.* **Peter** *goes up and stares at his mam through the open bedroom door.* **Margaret** *doesn't turn round.*

Margaret   Turn the lamp off, lovey, and go down.

Peter *does as he's told.*

Back in the living room, he picks up his glass of white rum and sits down in front of the TV.

The three males drink their glasses of white rum.

Printed in the United Kingdom
by Lightning Source UK Ltd.
123086UK00001B/167/A